The User's Guide to Everything You Need to Know About Cryptocurrency

LAWRENCE ALBRITTON

Co-Author Jonathan Banks

DEDICATION

Grandma Hattie - Motivation

Glory – For always knowing my potential

Jonathan J. Banks – ig: iGrowMoguls

Angel The Wizdom Flower

CONTENTS

PREFACE

THE REINTRODUCTION TO
THE REST OF YOUR LIFE

First, let me state that I am not a professional investor. Please do your own research. While it is evolving rapidly and shows promising potential, blockchain technology is still in its infancy. One day, I was discussing the importance of investing with a good friend when he grabbed my remote, hit the Netflix button, and we proceeded to watch *Banking on Bitcoin* (definitely a must-watch). The message was that this technology is a hedge against government failure and big corporate bailouts. That was when my knowledge of cryptocurrency and blockchain began. A week later, around September 2017, I watched the film again, and from there my curiosity continued to grow. I opened my first brokerage account with Fidelity in July 2017 and started investing in various companies on the stock market. The desire to learn and earn from investing eventually led me to investing in the greatest technological advance since the emergence of the Internet. Learning the skills required to invest in and understand blockchain technology can be an overwhelming process when we've conducted business transactions the same way for centuries. Change is the only constant; to disagree is to argue against growth. Repetition is the father of learning, and we must adjust to societal trends that can help us progress our lives.

Most people aren't aware of the emergence and importance of bitcoin and blockchain technology, which has led the way for thousands of other coins, such as ethereum and ripple. So, what is blockchain technology? A blockchain can be thought of as a decentralized database that can't be corrupted or destroyed, expanding the functions and improving the accountability of any entity that takes advantage of the system.

Here's what Wikipedia has to say about blockchain technology:

> "A blockchain, originally block chain, is a growing list of records, called blocks, that are linked using cryptography. Each block contains a cryptographic hash of the previous block, a timestamp, and transaction data (generally represented as a Merkle tree).
>
> By design, a blockchain is resistant to modification of the data. It is 'an open, distributed ledger that can record transactions between two parties efficiently and in a verifiable and permanent way'. For use as a distributed ledger, a blockchain is typically managed by a peer-to-peer network collectively adhering to a protocol for inter-node communication and validating new blocks. Once recorded, the data in any given block cannot be altered retroactively without alteration of all subsequent blocks, which requires consensus of the network majority. Although blockchain records are not unalterable, blockchains may be considered secure by design and exemplify a distributed computing system with high Byzantine fault tolerance. Decentralized consensus has therefore been claimed with a blockchain."
>
> Blockchain was invented by a person (or group of people) using the name Satoshi Nakamoto in 2008 to serve as the public transaction ledger of the cryptocurrency bitcoin. The identity of Satoshi Nakamoto is unknown. The invention of the blockchain for bitcoin made

it the first digital currency to solve the double-spending problem without the need of a trusted authority or central server. The bitcoin design has inspired other applications, and blockchains that are readable by the public are widely used by cryptocurrencies. Blockchain is considered a type of payment rail. Private blockchains have been proposed for business use. Sources such as *Computerworld* called the marketing of such blockchains without a proper security model 'snake oil'."

The purpose of this book is to show you an easy and secure way to purchase, profit from, and protect your digital currency. Don't be afraid of investing once you've gained the knowledge in this book. Fear is negative energy. Never be afraid to invest in what you're passionate about. In this book, you will learn how to apply methods from someone who has already gained and connected accounts in the blockchain. Businesses and consumers alike will benefit tremendously and profit from what blockchain technology offers. Proper research doesn't require a huge investment. Opportunities of this nature are rare, yet achievable. The sole purpose of this publication is to inform, inspire, and show you how to invest in the future.

Thank you, #SatoshiNakamoto. And thank you, readers. I appreciate you all for taking a chance with this book.

"Watch your thoughts, they become your words; watch your words, they become your actions; watch your actions, they become your habits; watch your habits, they become your character; watch your character, it becomes your destiny."

— **Lao Tzu**

1 TAKING THE LEAP

Existence constantly evolves. Change is the only universal constant! Resisting results in failure. How can you evolve without taking leaps, without shifting from your comfort zone? For years, I feared the internet due to my lack of knowledge. In 2008, my first purchase on the internet ended up being a scam, and I lost $3,000. I felt so betrayed. I stayed away from the internet for years until I became a business owner and started learning how to navigate and transact safely on the internet. I had to take that leap if I wanted to succeed. I exchanged my apprehension for determination. Preparation and research are vital for anything you want to succeed at. You have to have conviction, to possess a firm belief that you can adapt to our ever-evolving world. This technology is new and exciting, and with time and patience you can easily transition into the transacting and trading methods of the future. Knowledge is power, but it has no potency unless it's applied. It's human nature to fear what you don't understand, but resilience is in our DNA. I live with high blood pressure fueled by terrible anxiety. It's challenging to feel hopeless, misunderstood, alone, and sometimes so worried and nervous that you feel as if you're going to break into a million pieces.

Yet we still strive to progress, provide, and protect what is dear to us. So be extremely careful about what information you allow in, and over time your mental clarity will be an asset when the time arrives to make decisions in the interest of securing and profiting from cryptocurrency, whether in the short or the long term. I'm no expert, but it doesn't take an expert to learn the power of blockchain technology. Some people have asked why they should even get involved with cryptocurrency at all. Well, bitcoin sold at $0.08 in July 2010. As of December 2017, it's nearing $20,000! Bitcoin and various altcoins are proving that with proper business plans, blockchain technology companies are essential and will continue to produce unimaginable, groundbreaking technologies the world can't ignore. Amazon will one day be accepting bitcoin as a form of payment. This technology works and going back to the old way of functioning would be like trading your car for a bicycle. You'd be going back in time. Don't fear it, and don't fight it. The sooner you realize that this is the new way of living and earning, the better positioned you will be in the long run—and the race is just beginning. Everything I'm telling you comes from personal experience. My research and investments are all derived from hours upon hours of research and awaking each day to a new understanding and new possibilities. I feel it's the best time to be alive. Taking charge and putting your future in your own hands is empowering and can give you real freedom if you believe that things will one day be better. Maybe you're unsure how that will happen, but you've always had that feeling in your heart. And that's why you're reading this book. I'm no different than you. I just knew it was time to get out of that false comfort zone, become the best version of myself, and help anyone I could along the way.

We all know there's a more powerful version of ourselves beneath the fear, and that's why I wrote this guide: to walk you through the process and help you discover a new way of thinking.

2 REBIRTH

Cryptocurrency mania! I know it sounds foreign, which it should if you've never investigated it before. But learning the language of the crypto world is exciting. When I come to a new field, I like to understand as much as I can about what I'm considering investing in. This technology isn't just a monetary investment. Millions of jobs will be created for those willing to learn blockchain technology skills, providing great benefits and security. The power of gathering information is at your fingertips. One of my favorite websites for obtaining information is YouTube. While the content is limitless, not all of it is correct, so always consider sources when researching anything. Please keep in mind that all the information I'm giving you is based on my own research and experience. In this chapter, I'll define and discuss common terms to help familiarize you with cryptocurrency and blockchain technology. I frequently visit chat platforms like Telegram messenger and news sites like Cointelegraph to monitor the flow of information and ask questions. Never feel intimidated or think your question is bad or stupid. Most people are friendly and excited to share what they have learned to spread the message of this new phenomenon. New blogs and podcasts are created every day to expand our knowledge, with hundreds of crypto- and blockchain-related programs already available.

A few of my favorite podcasts are CryptoSpendthrift's Bitcoin and Cryptocurrency Podcast, The Bad Crypto Podcast, and Unchained, just to name a few, and I frequently visit informative sites like Reddit, ChainHub, BTCNews, and CryptoNews.pro. Once you research and dive into the brilliance of this technology of the future, you will clearly see that it has arrived! It doesn't take a college degree to see the rewards of using and understanding this technology if you simply dedicate a small part of your online activities to becoming more familiar with our future way of handling transactions. Knowing that you are capable of taking charge of your future will empower and inspire you.

What are digital currency and cryptocurrency exchanges?

Digital currency and cryptocurrency exchanges are businesses that allow customers to trade digital currencies or cryptocurrencies for other assets, such as conventional fiat currencies like US dollars or euros.

What are the different types of exchanges?

- **Trading Platforms** – These are websites that connect buyers and sellers and take a fee from each transaction.

- **Direct Trading** – These are platforms where individuals around the world can exchange currencies in direct person-to-person trades. Direct trading exchanges don't have a fixed marketplace price; instead, each seller sets their own exchange rate.

- **Brokers** – These are websites anyone can visit to buy cryptocurrencies at a price set by the broker. Cryptocurrency brokers are similar to foreign exchange dealers.

❖ Top American Cryptocurrency Exchanges

- **Coinbase** – Coinbase is the most popular and probably the fastest and easiest way to buy bitcoin, bitcoin cash, ethereum, ripple, litecoin, and dozens of other cryptocurrencies in the USA. Sign up and add a banking account or debit card to make purchases. Coinbase charges an additional fee for the use of debit cards, but you can get your coins immediately. Since I started writing this book, Coinbase has been insured by the FDIC, which means that if your funds are stolen due to Coinbase being hacked, your funds will be reimbursed up to

$250,000. I predict that the FDIC will insure more exchange sites soon.

- **Coinbase Pro** – Coinbase Pro is a more advanced version of the Coinbase exchange and also one the largest exchanges in the United States. Customers have various options to fund their accounts, including bank transfers, SEPA transfers, and bank wires, offering good prices and low fees. The interface can be difficult to navigate at first, but don't get discouraged.

- **CoinMama** – CoinMama enables people in pretty much every country on the globe to buy bitcoin using a credit or debit card. Again, additional fees apply, so compare rates on different exchanges.

- **Bittrex** – This is my personal favorite exchange! Bittrex is easy to adapt to. The exchange requires **two-factor authentication** for all withdrawals and API (application program interface) usage.

From here, I suggest doing some additional research to give you a broader understanding. Most importantly, take your time and develop your short- and long-term strategies. Keep in mind that your cryptocurrency should not be held in your exchange account after purchase. You should move it to a digital wallet or hardware wallet. Let's be real about this: we are here to profit from this technology. Protecting your digital assets should always be at the forefront of your mind when investing your hard-earned cash. .Monitoring the price and performance of cryptocurrencies is vital. Fortunately, it's also easy. The number of websites designed for this purpose is growing steadily. I use CoinMarketCap to check the price and market capitalization of each coin. There are other sites for this purpose, but CoinMarketCap is where I go to make sure a coin I'm interested in is legitimate.

One of the arts of investing is keeping a sharp eye on the market. Evaluating the price and market cap of an investment provides insight and clarity over time. Other sites for monitoring the market include Crypto Pro, Worldcoinindex, and CryptoCompare, just to name a few. I also strongly recommend becoming familiar with different cryptocurrencies' exchange rates by using a cryptocurrency converter. These tools convert the value of a selected cryptocurrency to the equivalent value of another cryptocurrency.

The process of purchasing cryptocurrency can be drastically slowed down when there is a sudden flood of transactions, which is an indication that the scaling system needs improvement. **What is scaling?** Scalability is the capability of a system, network, or process to handle an increasing number of transactions. A blockchain-related company can lose revenue if it lacks the capacity to facilitate fast transactions. Some companies implement **forks** to solve scaling issues. There are two types of forks: **soft forks** and **hard forks**. A soft fork is a change to the software protocol where only previously valid transactions are made invalid. A hard fork is a more aggressive change from the usual system because it makes previously invalid transactions valid, or vice versa. .I'm a member of the **Blockgeeks** community. Blockgeeks offers blockchain technology courses in addition to the option to chat and share ideas—no advertising allowed! This site contains tons of information on blockchain technology. I would encourage you to join the Blockgeeks community to increase your knowledge of blockchain technology. You may also have heard of dapps. **What are dapps?** A dapp is a decentralized application. Dapps use blockchain technology to decentralize different fields of activity, reducing the possibility of users being deceived or cheated and often increasing efficiency and user control.

There's one more term you should be familiar with: **smart contracts.** Smart contracts are similar to traditional contracts but differ in that they are written in computer code and are self-enforcing. One common use of smart contracts is to help you exchange currency or anything else of value in a transparent, conflict-free way while eliminating the middleman.

Being able to assess your **risk capacity and tolerance** is also very important when considering the future of your financial stability.

Blockchain technology is a wonderful puzzle to piece together because understanding one aspect motivates you to expand your knowledge in others.

3 CHARTING YOUR COURSE

Purchasing this guide puts you ahead of 99% of the population. You've acquainted yourself enough with the wealth of information about this new technology that you're now ready to think about improving the state of your own wealth. I know how you're feeling right now: to say that this could be the greatest technological moment in history is an understatement! This is a major groundbreaking opportunity to immerse yourself firmly in the future of financial security and a feeling of tremendous accomplishment. You've basically learned a new language. You've tapped in and introduced your mind to the new world right in front of you! Now you're wondering where to begin.

Let's start by getting an idea of how cryptocurrency works.

Most cryptocurrencies operate on a blockchain. A **blockchain** is a transactional database system duplicated several times across a network of computers around the world. A full copy of a cryptocurrency's blockchain contains every **transaction** ever executed in the cryptocurrency. With this information, you can find out how much value belonged to any **address** at any point in history. Transactions can't be corrupted or destroyed and are recorded forever.

People called **miners** use powerful computers to tally these transactions and secure the network. These are the people who run the blockchain. Their function is to update the blockchain each time a transaction is made to ensure the authenticity and accuracy of the information and to verify that each transaction has been processed correctly. This is the process of **cryptocurrency mining**, which can be very profitable, depending on whether you start out with a small investment or a large investment. You can mine individually or join a mining pool to increase your profits. You may want to take it to the next level and invest in a mining farm. Mining farms represent the new wave of mining on a large scale. A mining farm requires a lot of electricity, which can eat into your profits. If you're interested in mining, shop around for the equipment that suits you best and includes a superb installation and customer support team to ensure the proper set-up and housing of your investment.

An initial coin offering, or **ICO**, is a means by which funds are raised for a new cryptocurrency venture. ICOs are used by startups to avoid the tedious process involved in traditional start-up fundraising. There may be a specified target of capital required to fund projects. The so-called **Five Ts** for evaluating the potential success of a new company are **team, tech, token, technology, and timeline**. Companies that have created a prototype of their product tend to have more success than others because they are able to demonstrate that their product works. ICOs can be more profitable than other areas of cryptocurrency investing; investing in companies before they go public has enormous profit potential. Crafting a set of rules for what to expect from a possible investment is vital but not difficult to achieve. Just remember the **Five Ts**. Learning the difference between **utility tokens** and **security tokens** is an important part of deciding which coins you want to invest in. In short, utility tokens are used to pay for products and services, while owning a security token is essentially equivalent to owning shares of a corporation or business. Different coins, such as bitcoin and Ethereum, offer different technological solutions to today's complex problems. So, find your comfort level by passionately absorbing this world at your own pace.

The mental monster of anxiety will make you doubt what you know to be a wise investment decision. I'm speaking from years of experience of dealing with anxiety and being unaware that it was a real condition. Study what you're interested in when it comes to investing, and then just do it, because time is money. .Another important rule of investing is: "Don't invest what you can't afford to lose." If you focus and piece together the full functionality of this technology, you can profit and free yourself financially.

Note that I am not affiliated with any of the coins or companies I've mentioned so far.

The last investment opportunity I'm going to cover is **day trading**.

Day Trading

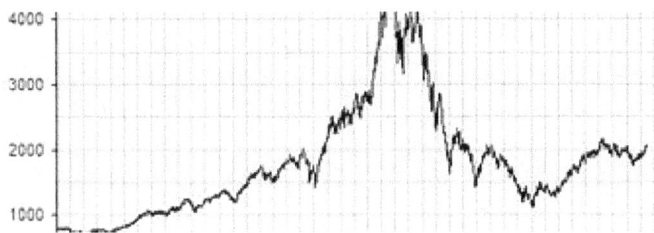

- Day trading is speculation in securities, specifically buying and selling financial instruments in the same trading day, such that all positions are closed before the market closes for the trading day. Traders who trade in this capacity with the motive of profit are therefore speculators. The methods of quick trading contrast with the long-term trades underlying buy-and-hold and value investing strategies. Day traders exit positions before the market closes to avoid unmanageable risks and negative price gaps between one day's close and the next day's price at the open.

- There is an abundance of books, courses, and websites to expand your day trading knowledge and skills.

- Exchanges like Binance and Bittrex are popular with day traders.

- **The risks are higher with day trading, so please do your research and only invest what is appropriate with the understanding that you may not produce the results expected. Be a responsible investor.**

I've only scratched the surface of the endless investment opportunities offered by blockchain technology. I feel privileged to share what I've learned, knowing it can benefit you greatly.

Let's move on to the next chapter, where we answer the biggest question so far...

4 WHAT'S IN IT FOR ME?

People invest for many reasons, but making money is certainly at the top of the list. Investing in this technology can potentially earn you a substantial amount of money for yourself and your retirement. Before we make an investment, we must first evaluate two things: our **risk capacity** and our **risk tolerance**. **Risk capacity** is knowing the amount of risk needed to achieve your goals. **Risk tolerance** is understanding your mental strength. Can you handle a potential profit loss in search of big gains? How comfortable are you when the market isn't doing as well as you expected? Anxiety can make things difficult and make you unsure of your decisions, but through research and proper diversification, you have the potential to financially secure a future for yourself and those you love.

Let's talk about **diversification**. It's important not to put all your eggs in one basket. This technology provides many ways for you to diversify your portfolio, whether you have short-, medium-, or long-term goals, and that's a beautiful thing. The type of investing you want to get involved with will determine the horizon of your investment level. Opportunities abound in the world of cryptocurrency and blockchain technology.

Understand the pros and cons of the investment you are about to make. Using multiple sources to obtain information will allow you to follow the trends and stay up to date on new and upcoming developments, which is vital. Your information sources are crucial, so visit a variety of different blogs and listen to as many cryptocurrency and blockchain podcasts as possible to expand your knowledge so you can distinguish legitimate projects from scams. This will help ease your anxiety when choosing your next investment opportunity. Find your comfort zone and focus on the new potential retirement options made available as a result of this technology. Everyone has to juggle the duties of everyday life, so there's nothing preventing you from taking the time to understand the new standards we must adapt to. Inflation is our enemy. The price of goods and services is increasing, while the value of the dollar is decreasing. Most employers don't increase the salary of their employees to help them maintain the same standard of living, with blockchain technology, we are entering a new dimension. Imagine if you could have had a stake in the internet when it first began? This is where we are now with the opportunity to invest early in blockchain.

The Emergence of Cryptocurrencies as Retirement Options

The Individual Retirement Account, or **IRA**, is one of the best investment options for earning money for your retirement. Today, IRAs can include cryptocurrencies.

The IRS-approved **Bitcoin IRA** was the first to offer this investment opportunity. Now ethereum, litecoin, ripple, and other digital currencies are also available, and there are several other cryptocurrency IRAs, including:

- Bitcoin IRA

- Goldco IRA

- Digital IRA

- Honestblock IRA

It's important to note that cryptocurrencies are considered property. IRS Notice 2014-21 states that virtual currencies are treated as property for US federal tax purposes. In short, cryptocurrencies can be taxed. I suggest speaking with an accountant about your cryptocurrency taxes.

The crypto craze is making retirement dreams come true every day. I would like to introduce a concept called the **50/15/5 Rule**. 50% of your income goes toward living expenses, 15% toward retirement, and 5% toward emergency savings. Yes, that only adds up to 70%; the remaining 30% can be used at your leisure. 30% can make a big difference in the crypto world.

Ask your employer if they are considering offering any of these great options. Get together with your family and do your research on how important it is for this technology to be part of your retirement portfolio. You can choose your own investments or have your advisor do it for you.

5 PROTECTING YOUR DIGITAL ASSETS

*"Biggest hack in history freezes $156 million
in digital currency funds."*
— Headline

*"$32 million dollars' worth of digital currency
Ether stolen by hackers."*
- CNBC

*"$64 million in cryptocurrency stolen
in sophisticated hack, exchange says."*
- Guardian

*"Identity thieves hijack cellphone accounts
to go after virtual currency."*
- New York Times

Hackers are widely feared—and for good reason. I want to discuss some of the layers of security important for protecting your digital information.

Antivirus Software

Purchasing good antivirus software is a good start. Antivirus software is used to prevent, detect, and remove malicious software. **Norton, Kaspersky, Webroot, Symantec, AVG, McAfee, and Bitdefenders** are just a few of the many options out there. So do your research and decide which antivirus software is best for you. Some provide protection for up to five devices, covering laptops, tablets, and smartphones.

Virtual Private Networks

One way for individual internet users to help secure their wireless transactions is by using a **virtual private network**, or VPN. VPNs enable users to connect to proxy servers for the purpose of protecting personal identity and location. Circumventing geo-restrictions is another benefit of using a VPN, but some sites will block access to VPN users.

Two-way Authentication

Two-way authentication provides an additional layer of security that makes it difficult for hackers to gain access to your devices and accounts. Apple uses two-way authentication. Google has an authenticator app that I use. I highly recommend downloading an authenticator app for your tablets and mobile devices.

Public Wi-Fi Dangers

Public Wi-Fi is often unsecured, posing a security risk. Recently, customers who visited a Starbucks in Buenos Aires were unaware of a 10-second delay put in place by a Starbucks worker that allowed him to mine cryptocurrency from their laptops when they were connected to the Starbucks Wi-Fi system. Imagine that. I'm literally shaking my head right now.

According to a survey conducted by Norton, most consumers are ignorant of the dangers of using public Wi-Fi. Hackers frequently take advantage of that ignorance. Using Wi-Fi in hotels and airports poses greater threats than using Wi-Fi at your home or workplace. It's literally impossible to know a good network from a bad one when connecting to public Wi-Fi and hotspots. Don't do your online banking or anything of a sensitive nature on a public Wi-Fi network.

Wallets, Private Keys, and Hardware Storage Devices

Once I started investing in cryptocurrency, I knew I needed to figure out where my cryptocurrency would reside.

Naturally, I **CryptoMaxx'd** the situation by confidently trusting Google to produce the best results to evaluate different cryptocurrency wallets. I prefer wallets that incorporate the private key option as an additional layer of security. *Investopedia* defines a private key as "a sophisticated form of cryptography that allows a user to access his or her cryptocurrency."

Everyone who uses a cryptocurrency has a public address and a private key for sending and receiving the cryptocurrency. The **public address** is where the funds are deposited and received. The **public key** is created via the **private key** through a complex mathematical algorithm. The private key ensures that you and only you have access to your funds. I know a lot of this sounds foreign but educating yourself and benefiting from this technology isn't difficult. The desire and ability to learn using this guide will ease the transition. These tools are here to protect us and going through the process is a lot easier than its sounds. Most of the information in this chapter is here to prepare you to make a very important decision: which type of wallet you want to use to store your cryptocurrency. The most used types of wallets are:

1. **Web/online wallets** – This type of wallet can only be accessed via the internet, not through a mobile app. It has a low rating for protecting your cryptocurrency because your information is kept by a third party, increasing the risk of your account being compromised.

2. **Desktop/mobile wallets** – These are applications you can download and install on your device. You can only access this kind of wallet from the device you download the app on. It is possible to restore your wallet on another device if it is damaged, lost, or stolen. This type of wallet can be better than a web/online wallet, depending on the security of the device you use.

3. **Hardware wallets** – This is my most trusted way of securely storing my cryptocurrency. It is also the

most popular solution others use for storing and securing their digital assets. Hardware wallets are encrypted devices that store your private keys. To access your wallet, you must insert the device into the USB port on your laptop and run the corresponding application, which is only accessible when the device is connected to a computer. This technology is growing every day, and more hardware wallets will be available by the time this book is published, but I am going to focus on the top four hardware wallets on the market right now.

1. **Ledger Blue** – According to www.ledgerwallet.com, the Ledger Blue, manufactured and designed in Paris, is "The most advanced hardware security device on the market. It boasts multi-application execution, and packs enterprise-level crypto-capabilities in a lightweight handheld device. It supports Bitcoin, Ethereum, and many other Altcoins designed around a Secure Element, featuring a touchscreen and USB & Bluetooth connectivity. Oversee and manage multiple accounts and addresses with the top-rated hardware cryptocurrency device on the market." It's currently out of stock on the Ledger website, where it sells for $269.99, but is priced up to $799 on sites like Amazon due to high demand. I'm currently registered and waiting to purchase the Ledger Blue's little brother, the next hardware wallet on this list.

2. **Ledger Nano S** – This hardware wallet is currently available online for $59, but more advanced versions can go for up to $150. The Ledger Nano S, like its big brother the Ledger Blue, supports bitcoin, Ethereum, and other altcoins in a highly secure system for storing your assets and making payments. The Nano S connects via USB to a computer and has a

secure OLED display for double-checking and confirming each transaction you make. You can also monitor your accounts and manage multiple cryptocurrency addresses from one device.

3. **KeepKey** – www.keepkey.com. KeepKey devices are designed and manufactured in Redmond, WA. At $18.89, KeepKey is cheaper on Amazon than on the KeepKey website itself, where it sells for $49. KeepKey supports bitcoin, ethereum, ripple, litecoin, and several other altcoins. KeepKey requires downloading and installing the KeepKey client app from the Google Chrome web store. Once connected via USB cable, just open Chrome, locate the KeepKey Client App, and secure your cryptocurrency assets.

4. **Trezor** – shop.trezor.io is the website to purchase this device, with models starting at $55. It is said to be the original and most secure hardware wallet and is manufactured in Russia. It is a highly sought-after hardware wallet, ranking among the top hardware cryptocurrency storage devices. Like the others, Trezor is mentioned in reputable news outlets for the security it offers. Some surveys rank Trezor higher than I do, but as a military veteran, the location of the manufacture and design of the device I choose to use is important to me, since war is waged on many fronts and cyberattacks are an ever-present threat to America. Let me be clear: in the interests of America and capitalism, you must do your own due diligence.

6 EFFICIENTLY PROCURING CRYPTOCURRENCY

Honestly, at the beginning of my journey, even after all the research I did online—visiting the official websites of the digital assets I was considering investing in; using social media sites like Facebook, Twitter, LinkedIn, and Instagram; interacting on forums like Telegram; reading cryptocurrency and blockchain news outlets and blogs; and keeping journals on multiple mobile devices, legal pads, notebooks, and printouts—I was still nervous. Even knowing that I had taken all the proper precautions to conduct an error-free transaction on my first attempt—I was still nervous .Despite my nervousness, not only was I successful with my first transaction, but I've been error-free in all my transactions since, mainly because I have no money to waste. In testing the reliability of this new technological investment opportunity, you must pay close attention to the details when conducting transactions. The odds of recovering your digital assets if you make an error are extremely low. Begin by researching different exchanges and evaluating them to determine which ones are best for you. Once you identify the right exchange, it's time to register an account. Get familiar with a couple of different exchanges, and when you feel comfortable enough, perform a small transaction or transfer some funds to another exchange. After that, you've made it through your first Cryptoland transaction process.

The important thing is to trust your knowledge in order to invest without losing your money. Getting into the habit of double checking the address when you send or receive cryptocurrency will prove to be a valuable trait in Cryptoland. The rush and excitement of this new technology can easily result in errors, such as sending a cryptocurrency to the wrong address.

I've sent bitcoin, ethereum, and litecoin from Coinbase to Bittrex, **Metamask**, and **Exodus**. Each exchange or wallet will show you which cryptocurrencies they support. If you want to send bitcoin from one exchange or wallet to another, for example, make sure you send it to the bitcoin address of the receiving exchange or wallet, not the address of any other cryptocurrency. Different wallets and exchanges support different cryptocurrencies, and most are adding more on a constant basis.

In my view, this technology has been waiting for people to become conscious of the chance to take control of their destiny and live the new American dream. Applying all this information is the key to evolving. Remember to take things at your own pace. Follow up and do your own research. If you have a problem, find the answer. For example, one day you may notice that your transactions are taking longer than normal to process. **Volatility and scaling operations** are potential causes. Learn about these potential causes so you know what's going on and you don't panic. Most mistakes are made when you become unsure of yourself. So always keep your risk tolerance and risk capacity safeguards at the forefront of your mind, while positioning yourself with the 50/15/5 strategy to make strong investments on the crypto chessboard that blockchain technology has made possible.

7 CRYPTO BRANDING

Lights, camera, action! Now you can see the many extraordinary opportunities in Cryptoland. By now, you should have formulated a plan and found an area of interest. The investment opportunities provided by this world-changing technology you have now been introduced to can be overwhelming. It can feel like we're living in the future. I talk about this everywhere I go, asking people if they have heard of bitcoin or cryptocurrency. Most haven't, so I feel it is my duty to inform those who are unaware of this opportunity to potentially change their lives forever. Together, we have now begun to fill in the gaps in fully understanding the amazing possibilities of our growing technology industry. I consider it my personal mission to share the importance of blockchain technology with everyone. Basing our future transactions and conversations on blockchain technology is one of the best life decisions we can make. This technology has the power to revive impoverished nations, so imagine what we can do in our own communities. This technology is our ticket, our wake-up call to immerse ourselves in the computer-code world of blockchain greatness.

An aspect of blockchain we haven't considered yet is careers. When it comes to careers, those of us who are self-employed are developing businesses and brands, and blockchain technology can help us thrive in this area. Let's take a look at a company called **Tesloop**. Tesloop is the world's first sustainable mobility company and has partnered with a company I am invested in called **Simple Token**. Simple Token makes it easy for companies to create their own token on the Simple Token platform, and the company is building on new tokenization concepts all the time. Tesloop began operating in June 2015 in California and is the most rapidly growing mobility service. The company offers mobility services in the form of electric semi-autonomous vehicles and plans to expand its fleet to include Tesla vehicles. In just two years, Tesloop has become the world's highest-rated transportation company. In 2018, Tesloop expanded its offerings to create a single service to replace all consumer vehicle interactions, including car ownership, carpooling, and rental services.

The future of careers, technology, and investing has arrived. Tesloop is just one example of how our world is changing right before our eyes. Throughout this book, you have learned the language of blockchain and the connections between its different parts. Now take what you've learned as you start your blockchain investment journey and share it with others—every experience, every innovation, everything that will help you and those after you keep this technology thriving. Stay current and stay in tune with what's going on in the market. I am on a level beyond excitement. In my view, the overall assessment by traditional news outlets hasn't promoted the value of blockchain technology. I am deeply invested and currently profiting from this technology every day on many different levels. I wrote this book to teach the world that this is possible and can be a means to a better way of life. Blockchain technology will be our new standard and our shield against inflation.

This technology benefits every sector of our lives. If you've read this far, there's no need to repeat myself, because you've researched enough to validate the truth of what I'm sharing. There are periods in history that have impacted civilization forever because they were designed to help us progress, and this is one of them.

Some words of advice: Be open to what you don't know. Be open and curious. Allow the flow of information to help you evolve. Ask questions. Don't believe the hype about mental imprisonment, and don't fear leaving your comfort zone. Miseducation, politics, family structure—take your pick. No more excuses; you are going to get back up and keep climbing that hill. We will never settle again, never give up, never stop striving to be the best version of ourselves. Our existence here is temporary, but not the end—so grow, prosper, and remind this planet that life is what you make it. My righteous cry was heard when #SatoshiNakamoto decentralized the world. Creating blessings is my motivation, and I want to sincerely thank you for reading and allowing your mind to expand beyond its present understanding. I'm confident that the knowledge I've shared from my research and experience will benefit you. In fact, it will enrich every aspect of your life. History is what you make it—so get off the sidelines.

ABOUT THE AUTHOR

Always imaginatively connected to the world of business technology, Sir Lawrence Albritton is a former naval aviation plane captain and is now a licensed FAA remote pilot and the owner of Eye Sky Phantoms Inc., a US-based, veteran-owned drone service provider. Lawrence has quickly become a trusted and reliable source when it comes to the benefits of investing in blockchain technology. He has been featured in national and international publications, including popular titles such as BrandedMag.us and The411Magazine.com, as a top resource contributor and is currently listed in the largest veteran database for entrepreneurial service members.

A huge motivational factor in Lawrence's everyday drive is derived from his desire to connect people with life-changing information they are unaware of. Currently, he is building a foundation for women's empowerment while working in other sectors to create new school scholarships through smart contracts. As an AMVETS member, his patriotism and support for the Wounded Warrior Project continues to build his strong relationship with other vets and service members. In his spare time, you can find Lawrence traveling and speaking all over the nation, spreading knowledge, love, and wealth-building ideals everywhere he can.

ACKNOWLEDGEMENTS

The Trump Administration

Ripple

Vitalik Buterin

Ian Balina

Digital Asset Investor

I Am Legion

BTC News

Bad Crypto Podcast

www.ingramcontent.com/pod-product-compliance
Lightning Source LLC
Chambersburg PA
CBHW072048230526
45468CB00019B/1050